BIOGRAPHIC
AUSTEN

BIOGRAPHIC
AUSTEN

SOPHIE COLLINS

AMMONITE
PRESS

First published 2017 by
Ammonite Press
an imprint of Guild of Master Craftsman Publications Ltd
Castle Place, 166 High Street, Lewes, East Sussex, BN7 1XU,
United Kingdom

ISBN 978 1 78145 292 9

Publisher: Jason Hook
Concept Design: Matt Carr
Design & Illustration: Matt Carr & Robin Shields
Editor: Jamie Pumfrey
Consultant Editor: Dr Emma Clery
Picture Research: Hedda Roennevig

Colour reproduction by GMC Reprographics
Printed and bound in China

CONTENTS

ICONOGRAPHIC

WHEN WE CAN RECOGNIZE A WRITER BY
A SET OF ICONS, WE CAN ALSO RECOGNIZE
HOW COMPLETELY THAT WRITER AND THEIR
WORK HAVE ENTERED OUR CULTURE
AND OUR CONSCIOUSNESS.

INTRODUCTION

It was the (now almost forgotten) literary critic George Saintsbury who coined the term 'Janeite' for a lover of Austen's novels – he was writing the introduction, in 1894, to a new edition of *Pride and Prejudice*. At the time, she had already become far, far more popular than she had ever been during her lifetime. And 'Janeite' quickly became the term for readers who go beyond enthusiasm. Today, Austen is not only loved but idolized by legions of fans. This can lead to her being pigeonholed as a romantic novelist – and discussed as such in the dozens of societies, blogs and books dedicated to her work and life – but to define her so narrowly is to miss out.

Which Jane Austen her readers meet in her works depends on which Austen they choose to see. Her books present several different personalities: is she the charming author of romances, the sharp, humorous observer of social mores, or the cynic who looks out sometimes from behind some of her bleaker or more ironic passages?

"WALTER SCOTT HAS NO BUSINESS TO WRITE NOVELS, ESPECIALLY GOOD ONES. – IT IS NOT FAIR. – HE HAS FAME AND PROFIT ENOUGH AS A POET, AND SHOULD NOT BE TAKING THE BREAD OUT OF OTHER PEOPLE'S MOUTHS."

Of course the answer is that she is all of them. Her fiercer critics have tended to miss the point: in a limited landscape – the famous "three or four families in a country village" that she recommended to her niece Anna as the best focus for a novelist – she created a world of variety, and one that repays repeated rereading. Charlotte Brontë may have carped that she would "hardly like to live with [Austen's] ladies and gentlemen, in their elegant but confined houses", and Mark Twain was even more forthright, elevating his dislike of Austen's ladylike qualities into a tongue-in-cheek literary loathing, but no-one has ever been better at capturing the atmosphere of a conversation, or the echo of feelings that can't be spoken. And those feelings are often far from romantic clichés.

Material that contains so many layers remains enjoyable, but it can still be hard to see something so familiar – from the original books to the multiple blogs and films – from a fresh angle. One way to enhance a visit is to take another look at Austen's circumstances – the world she was born into and the ways in which it changed during the course of her brief lifetime; the nuts and bolts of her life and what she made of it; and the legacy she left. The *Biographic* treatment offers an ideal opportunity for coming at the subject obliquely: it's partly a life-in-numbers (How many brothers and sisters? How many moves around the country? How many books, and how did they compare with those of her contemporaries? How much money?), and partly the chance to look at elements in multiple contexts, past and present.

"I MUST KEEP TO MY OWN STYLE AND GO ON IN MY OWN WAY; AND THOUGH I MAY NEVER SUCCEED AGAIN IN THAT, I AM CONVINCED THAT I SHOULD TOTALLY FAIL IN ANY OTHER."

This book isn't designed to be read in order. Flip through the pages and the visual hooks will pull you in. Along the way, you'll discover Jane Austen in different settings: as a Georgian, as a sister, as an invalid, as an author keen both for publication and for royalties, and even, on occasion, as a shrew. Austen herself was a realist and it's this, above her other qualities, that makes her seem recognizable to us – she certainly knew that life wasn't all roses. She was perhaps the first novelist to catch the true flavour of everyday life, with its peaks and troughs and mundanities, and in this she remains unassailable.

"MRS HALL, OF SHERBORNE, WAS BROUGHT TO BED YESTERDAY OF A DEAD CHILD... OWING TO A FRIGHT. I SUPPOSE SHE HAPPENED UNAWARES TO LOOK AT HER HUSBAND..."

JANE AUSTEN

01
LIFE

"COMPOSITION SEEMS TO ME IMPOSSIBLE WITH A HEAD FULL OF JOINTS OF MUTTON AND DOSES OF RHUBARB."

—Jane Austen, letter to Cassandra Austen on
the difficulties of writing in everyday life, 1816

JANE AUSTEN

was born on 16 December 1775 in Steventon, Hampshire, England

STEVENTON

HAMPSHIRE

Jane Austen was born on 16 December 1775 in the rectory in the small Hampshire village of Steventon, where her father, John Austen, was vicar. Either Jane was sluggish coming into the world or her mother, Cassandra Austen, had made a mistake in her dates – she arrived a full month later than expected. The seventh of eight children, she was the younger of only two daughters in the brood.

The rectory had seven bedrooms and three attics, and when all the family were at home, as well as at least two servants, it was crowded but cheerful. However, like many other ladies in the late 18th century, Mrs Austen didn't keep her new babies with her: at around three months old they were sent to board with a wet nurse in the village. There they stayed for at least a year, with regular visits from their parents, before returning home as toddlers. It was the unsentimental but practical routine of a busy vicar's wife of limited means.

UNITED KINGDOM

Also born in ▶
Hampshire:
Charles Dickens
(1812–70)

NEWFOUNDLAND

A violent hurricane, later named the 'Independence Hurricane', hits the colony of Newfoundland, killing more than 4,000 people.

BOSTON

In America, the battles of Lexington and Concord, fought in Massachusetts County and Boston, mark the first military engagement of the Revolution on 19 April, the day after Paul Revere's legendary ride to warn of the British approach.

THE WORLD IN 1775

PHILADELPHIA

The first anti-slavery society is founded. Thomas Paine is among its thirty members, the majority of whom were Quakers.

The rural England Jane Austen was born into in the last quarter of the 18th century was deceptively peaceful. Beyond the walls of the Steventon rectory, however, the Industrial Revolution was already under way, and the first battle of the American War of Independence had been fought. Captain Cook had made his first voyage of discovery to Australia a few years earlier. In adulthood Austen might concentrate on her close-ups, the "little bit (two inches wide) of ivory" on which she chose to work, but the outside world would make its incursions, both into her life and even, sometimes, into her books.

BIRMINGHAM

In England, James Watt completes the designs for his first two industrial, working 'atmospheric pressure' engines.

BIRMINGHAM

John Baskerville, eminent English typographer and printer, dies in Birmingham on 8 January.

ST PETERSBURG

In Russia, on 17 March, Catherine the Great issues an edict forbidding freed serfs from being returned to serfdom.

PORTSMOUTH

Captain James Cook returns from his second voyage on HMS *Resolution*, anchoring off the southern coast of England, having crossed the Antarctic Circle for the first time.

REIMS

On 11 June, Louis XVI and Marie Antoinette, the last king and queen of France, are crowned in Reims Cathedral.

Reverend
Thomas Leigh
(1696–1764)

Jane Walker
(1704–68)

William Austen
(1701–37)

Rebecca
Hampson
(dates unknown)

Cassandra Leigh
(1739–1827)

Reverend
George Austen
(1731–1805)

James Austen
(1765–1819)

George Austen
(1766–1838)

Edward Austen
adopted,
became Knight
after 1812
(1767–1852)

Henry Thomas
Austen
(1771–1850)

 girl (Jane's niece)

boy (Jane's nephew)

JANE'S FAMILY TREE

Somehow the picture of Jane Austen that has been passed down is that of a single lady in a quiet room, daily scratching away with a quill. But a quick look at her diary and her family proves this to be very far from the truth. Of her seven siblings, not only did all survive into adulthood, but five married and four of those had extensive families. Francis Austen and Edward Austen-Knight had 11 children each, most of whom also lived to adulthood – unusual at the time. Austen was surrounded by family, and went on rounds of visits to family and friends constantly. She often lamented that it was difficult to find time to write.

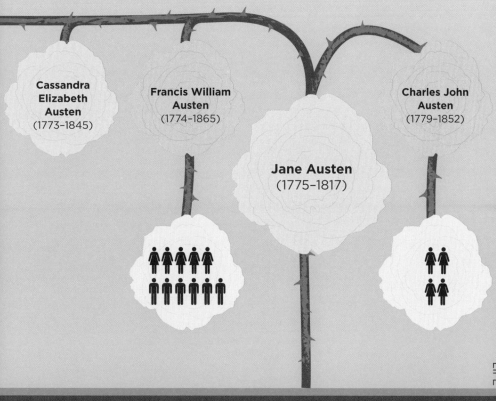

Cassandra Elizabeth Austen (1773–1845)

Francis William Austen (1774–1865)

Jane Austen (1775–1817)

Charles John Austen (1779–1852)

AUSTEN MINOR: THE EARLY YEARS

Jane Austen wrote from childhood, but the first of her novels to be published – *Sense and Sensibility* – did not appear until 1811, when she was 35, 14 years after her father had first approached a publisher on her behalf. She came from a household in which self-expression was commonplace: her mother wrote notes in rhyme to her children and to the boys who boarded at the rectory, and all the children took part in regular family theatricals. Home for the Austen family was a lively, energetic place, full of incident.

1787

Jane begins to write in earnest, working on the stories and poems that would later become known as her juvenilia.

1786

Vathek, the Gothic masterpiece of William Thomas Beckford, is translated into English and published.

1785

Jane and Cassandra are sent to the Abbey School at Reading, run by Madame La Tournelles. There, they learn spelling and grammar, needlework, some French and music. They return home in 1786.

1784

The Austen family puts on a performance of Sheridan's *The Rivals* for family and friends.

1783

Jane and Cassandra are sent to school at Mrs Cawley's establishment in Oxford. When the school moves to Southampton shortly afterwards, typhoid fever breaks out there and the girls return to Steventon.

1775

Jane Austen is born on 16 December at Steventon Rectory.

1778

Fanny Burney's *Evelina*, a novel about an ingenue's entry into the world, is published and becomes popular.

1782

The first family theatrical performance takes place at the Rectory. Jane is just six years old.

1790

Jane writes her first longer work, entitled *Love and Freindship* (sic).

1793

The pace of writing picks up. Jane writes the last item of her juvenilia.

1794

Jane begins work on *Lady Susan* and *Elinor and Marianne*.

1794

Ann Radcliffe's *The Mysteries of Udolpho*, given a comic starring role in *Northanger Abbey*, is published.

1795

Jane has her only real love affair, with Tom Lefroy, the nephew of family friends. The friendship is discouraged by their families, and early in 1796 Tom leaves Steventon. Jane never sees him again.

1796

Fanny Burney's third novel, *Camilla*, is published, financed by subscription. Jane's name is on the subscribers' list.

1796

Jane begins the novel called *First Impressions*, which will become *Pride and Prejudice*.

1803

Jane's brother Henry submits the manuscript of *Susan* to Crosby & Company in London, who purchase the copyright for £10. Benjamin Crosby promises to publish the book, but without committing to a date (he never does so).

1802

In December, Jane receives her only proposal of marriage – from Harris Bigg-Wither, a childhood friend. Heir to a substantial estate, he is described as unattractive; she accepts, but changes her mind the following day.

1800

George Austen announces his retirement and his intention to move his family to Bath.

1798

Jane completes revisions on *Elinor and Marianne*, which will become *Sense and Sensibility*, and begins a new novel, known sequentially first as *Susan* and then as *Catherine*, which will finally be published as *Northanger Abbey*.

1797

George Austen submits a letter of enquiry for Jane's work to London publisher Thomas Cadell; the letter is returned unopened. Jane and Cassandra spend some time visiting their brother James in Bath.

DAUGHTERS OF THE RECTORY

Jane Austen and the Brontë sisters are probably the best-known parsons' daughters in English literature. Between the four of them, they produced a baker's dozen of novels, including some of the most enduringly popular in the English language. Austen came first – she died just a year before Charlotte Brontë was born. However, although their lives have a superficial likeness – of the four, only Charlotte married, and then comparatively late in life – the experiences of Austen and the Brontës were as different from each other as the rolling, pretty terrain of Hampshire is from the harsh, rough landscape of the Yorkshire moors and the tough little towns set on them. The Brontës were also further down the social scale than Austen – they had less time to write, and their experiences of life were more independent. Perhaps the most surprising aspect of all the authors is quite how much, in the course of brief and restrictive lives, they managed to produce.

TOTAL WORDS: 732,049

PRIDE AND PREJUDICE 122,685

SENSE AND SENSIBILITY 123,623

NORTHANGER ABBEY 77,977

EMMA 162,853

MANSFIELD PARK 160,802

PERSUASION 84,109

JANE AUSTEN (1775–1817)

Other works
Juvenilia

Pseudonym
4 novels published as 'A Lady'

Northanger Abbey and *Persuasion* published posthumously under her own name

AUSTEN

CHARLOTTE BRONTË (1816–55)

Other works
Juvenilia

Collection of poems
(with her sisters)

Pseudonym
Published under the
name of Currer Bell

EMILY BRONTË (1818–48)

Other works
Juvenilia

Collection of poems
(with her sisters)

Pseudonym
Published under the
name of Ellis Bell

ANNE BRONTË (1820–49)

Other works
Juvenilia

Collection of poems
(with her sisters)

Pseudonym
Published under the
name of Acton Bell

TOTAL WORDS:
1,043,451

JANE EYRE 186,418

SHIRLEY 204,465

VILLETTE 192,772

THE PROFESSOR 87,912

WUTHERING HEIGHTS 136,604

AGNES GREY 67,834

THE TENANT OF WILDFELL HALL 167,446

LIFE

THE WRITE STUFF: AUSTEN'S ADULTHOOD

Austen's five years in Bath, from 1801, did not prove productive, although she was to put her experiences there to good use later. A year or two of constant moving followed her father's death, but when her brother Frank offered Jane, Mrs Austen and Cassandra a house at Chawton, the three settled into a steady life. It was at Chawton that Jane would enjoy a burst of creativity, boosted when *Sense and Sensibility* finally made it into print in 1811. She must have been gratified, too, to have had *Emma* accepted by John Murray, 'the civil rogue' and the stellar publisher of his age. Sadly, after a lengthy period of illness, which has today's experts arguing to diagnose, she died in 1817. *Northanger Abbey* and *Persuasion* were published posthumously later that year.

1810
Thomas Egerton accepts *Sense and Sensibility* for publication.

1809
Jane challenges Benjamin Crosby over his failure to publish *Susan*. He tells her to buy the copyright back but she cannot afford to.

1808
Francis offers Mrs Austen and his sisters a house at Chawton to serve as their permanent home.

1804
Jane begins work on a new novel, *The Watsons*. It will never be completed. She spends most of the summer on a visit to Lyme Regis.

1806
Austen, Cassandra and her mother move constantly – visiting Manydown Park, Bath and Warwickshire. Subsequently they move to Southampton to stay with Francis Austen.

1805
George Austen dies suddenly; Cassandra and Jane move to lodgings in Gay Street in Bath.

1811

Jane starts work on *Mansfield Park*. *Sense and Sensibility* is finally published to good reviews.

1817

Jane begins work on *The Brothers* (later published as *Sanditon*). By April, Jane is unwell and confined to bed. She writes her will. On 18 July, Jane Austen dies. She is buried in the north aisle of Winchester Cathedral. *Northanger Abbey* and *Persuasion* are published by John Murray. For the first time, Austen's work is published under her own name.

1812

First Impressions is revised and sold to Thomas Egerton for £110.

1813

First Impressions is published as *Pride and Prejudice*. Second editions of both *Pride and Prejudice* and *Sense and Sensibility* are published before the end of the year.

1816

Susan is reclaimed from Benjamin Crosby; the title is changed first to *Catherine* and ultimately to *Northanger Abbey*. Henry Austen's business fails. Jane becomes ill, but continues to work on *The Eliots*.

1814

Mansfield Park is published in May and the first edition sells out by October.

1815

Jane finishes *Emma* and starts *The Eliots*, which will become *Persuasion*. *Emma* is accepted by John Murray, one of the most esteemed publishers in London; the Prince Regent requests a dedication in her next work. Despite her distaste, Jane dedicates *Emma* to him.

AUSTEN'S LAPTOP

Not only did Jane Austen write novels, but like most ladies of her day, she was also a prolific correspondent. So she spent many, many hours in the physical act of writing. Cassandra Austen destroyed many letters after her death and excised a number of others – the gentle author of the novels could be surprisingly shrewish when it came to neighbours and relations, and her sister was probably aiming to keep her reputation intact. But what did she write with, and on what?

LAP DESK

A small, portable desk, which both acted as storage for writing materials and provided a gently sloping surface to write on, was a commonplace object used by both ladies and gentlemen.

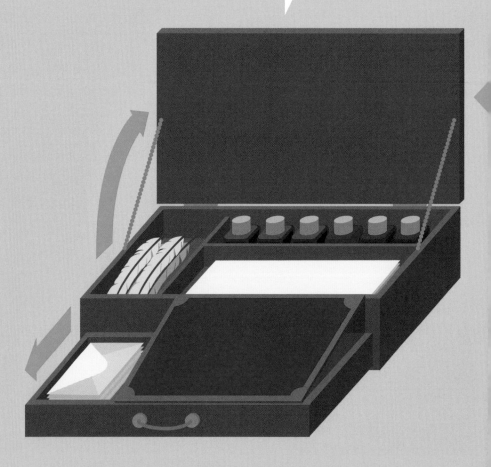

PENS

Although metal pen nibs existed by the time Austen was writing, they were more expensive than quills. Writing quills were usually made from goose feathers. Complaints about one's pen were commonplace in letters and journals.

Take goose feathers. | Heat feathers to harden. | Carefully cut to make a nib.

INK

Ink, too, was cheaper to make at home. Martha Lloyd's recipe for ink still exists, and this is probably the same one that Jane used.

4oz of blue gauls

2oz of green copperas

1½oz of gum arabic

"Break the gauls. The gum and copperas must be beaten in a mortar and put into a pint of strong stale beer; with a pint of small beer. Put in a little refin'd sugar. It must stand in the chimney corner fourteen days and be shaken two or three times a day."

GAULS gallic acid, made from oak apples

COPPERAS iron sulphate

SMALL BEER weak, diluted beer, different to 'strong', or regular, beer

PAPER

Austen not only made her own mini-books by folding several sheets of paper together but also wrote in ready-made books, quarto-sized, purchased from a stationer. In wealthier circles, letters and notes might be written on elegant paper – in *Pride and Prejudice*, sneering Miss Bingley writes on "a sheet of elegant, little, hot-pressed paper". This would be made entirely from rag fibre, and heated before being pressed flat – giving it a smooth surface, easy to write on.

AN EXOTIC COUSIN

'Abroad' doesn't feature a great deal in the books of Jane Austen. France, England's sworn enemy, gets a total of just three mentions in her work, all in *Northanger Abbey*. It's easy to come to the conclusion that her surroundings were quite parochial and her immediate social circle very safe, so it comes as a surprise to learn that one of Jane's favourite cousins – ultimately, also to become her sister-in-law – was the very exotic Eliza, Comtesse de Feuillide.

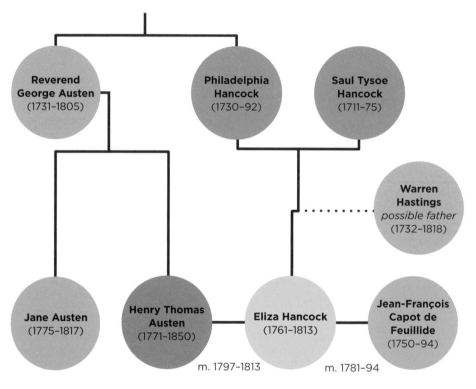

Reverend George Austen (1731–1805)

Philadelphia Hancock (1730–92)

Saul Tysoe Hancock (1711–75)

Warren Hastings
possible father
(1732–1818)

Jane Austen (1775–1817)

Henry Thomas Austen (1771–1850)

Eliza Hancock (1761–1813)

Jean-François Capot de Feuillide (1750–94)

m. 1797–1813   m. 1781–94

1761

BIRTH

Eliza is born to Philadelphia Hancock in Calcutta, India. She is given the Hancock name, though it is rumoured that her godfather, Warren Hastings, was her real father.

1768

Eliza travels with her mother to London, where she lives for some years. Hancock remains in India, where he dies in 1775.

Eliza is said to have been a source of inspiration for the creation of Mary Crawford – charming, charismatic, but morally suspect – in *Mansfield Park*.

1813

Henry brings Jane to London to stay with her sick sister-in-law. On 27 April, Eliza dies, much mourned by Jane.

1794

'Count' de Feuillide is guillotined in Paris by the revolutionaries.

1797

Eliza accepts Henry Austen, 10 years her junior, who has been pressing her to marry him for some time.

1790

Eliza returns to England after the French Revolution begins.

1786

Eliza, pregnant, visits her Austen relations in England. She stays for over a year, charming the young Austens. Her tales of high society prompt increasingly sophisticated theatricals at Steventon.

1778

The widowed Philadelphia takes her 17-year-old daughter to Paris, where they are accepted into society and attend the court at Versailles. Pretty and lively, Eliza is a social success.

1781

Eliza marries French army officer Jean-François Capot de Feuillide.

LOOKS LIKE JANE?

Jane Austen does not seem to have been vain about her appearance. She was born a good 60 years before the invention of photography, and we have only the tiny sketch by Cassandra to identify her by. Later described by Jane's niece, Anna Lefroy, as "hideously unlike" it certainly doesn't accord very closely with the many descriptions by her contemporaries. So what did Austen really look like? Here are a handful of clues from her friends and family – and at least a few of the elements overlap.

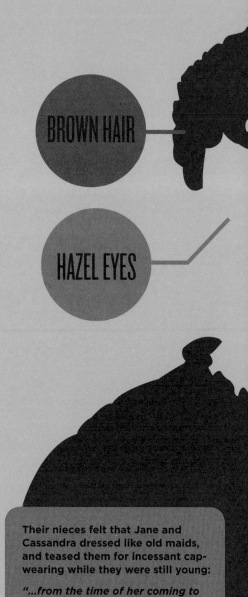

BROWN HAIR

HAZEL EYES

"SHE WAS TALL AND SLENDER, HER FACE WAS ROUNDED WITH A CLEAR BRUNETTE COMPLEXION AND BRIGHT HAZEL EYES. HER CURLY BROWN HAIR ESCAPED ALL ROUND HER FOREHEAD..."

—Edward Austen Leigh, nephew

"SHE WAS FAIR AND HANDSOME, SLIGHT AND ELEGANT, WITH CHEEKS A LITTLE TOO FULL."

—Sir Egerton Bridges, family friend in Austen's youth

Their nieces felt that Jane and Cassandra dressed like old maids, and teased them for incessant cap-wearing while they were still young:

"...from the time of her coming to live at Chawton she always wore a cap, except when her nieces had her in London and forbade it."

—Edward Austen Leigh, nephew of Jane

QUITE
TALL

ALWAYS
WORE A CAP

ROUND FACE

"HER FACE WAS RATHER ROUND THAN LONG, SHE HAD... A CLEAR BROWN COMPLEXION, AND VERY GOOD HAZEL EYES. HER HAIR, A DARKISH BROWN, CURLED NATURALLY, IT WAS IN SHORT CURLS AROUND HER FACE."

—Caroline Austen, niece

"HER STATURE RATHER EXCEEDED THE MIDDLE HEIGHT... HER FEATURES WERE SEPARATELY GOOD... HER COMPLEXION OF THE FINEST TEXTURE..."

—Henry Austen, brother

WHAT'S WRONG WITH JANE?

Doctors have long debated the nature of the illness that carried Austen off at the age of only 41. Sir Zachary Pope's paper on her health, written in 1964, sought to establish that she had died of Addison's disease, but in 2004 a new take on Austen's health was published by Annette Upfal at the University of Queensland. It threw a different complexion on the author's final illness.

Jane Austen was ill for about 18 months before she died. Her letters record some symptoms – in her own words:

8 September 1816

"MY BACK HAS GIVEN ME SCARCELY ANY PAIN FOR MANY DAYS..."

16 December 1816

"I WAS FORCED TO DECLINE [AN INVITATION TO DINNER], THE WALK IS BEYOND MY STRENGTH..."

January 1817

"I AM MORE AND MORE CONVINCED THAT BILE IS AT THE BOTTOM OF ALL I HAVE SUFFERED..."

23 March 1817

"I HAVE HAD A GOOD DEAL OF FEVER... BETTER NOW, AND RECOVERING MY LOOKS A LITTLE, WHICH HAVE BEEN BAD ENOUGH, BLACK AND WHITE AND EVERY WRONG COLOUR..."

6 April 1817

"I HAVE BEEN SUFFERING FROM A BILIOUS ATTACK WITH A GOOD DEAL OF FEVER..."

22 May 1817

"AN ATTACK OF MY SAD COMPLAINT SEIZED ME... THE MOST SEVERE I EVER HAD...MY CHIEF SUFFERINGS WERE FROM FEVERISH NIGHTS, WEAKNESS AND LANGUOR."

20 July 1817 (Cassandra Austen in a letter)

"... SHE WAS SEIZED AGAIN WITH THE SAME FAINTNESS... MR LYFORD [THE SURGEON] HAD APPLIED SOMETHING TO GIVE HER EASE AND SHE WAS IN A STATE OF QUIET INSENSIBILITY..."

Hodgkin's Lymphona, first considered in 2004, is the only condition that would meet all the symptoms.

CONDITION

SYMPTOMS	TUBERCULOSIS	STOMACH CANCER	ADDISON'S DISEASE	HODGKIN'S LYMPHOMA
Discolouration of the skin		✓	✓	✓
Attacks of faintness				✓
Back pain				✓
"Bilious attacks" (sickness and vomiting)	✓		✓	✓
"Languor" (all-round weakness)	✓	✓	✓	✓

FINAL RESTING PLACE

Jane Austen died on 18 July 1817 at number 8, College Street, Winchester, a rented house where she had gone to consult Mr Lyford, a Winchester surgeon, when the local doctor at Alton could no longer help her. She was buried in the nave of Winchester Cathedral. Her memorial stone, which lauds her character and her intellect, makes no mention of her writing.

IN MEMORY OF JANE AUSTEN, YOUNGEST DAUGHTER OF THE LATE REVD GEORGE AUSTEN, FORMERLY RECTOR OF STEVENTON IN THIS COUNTY. SHE DEPARTED THIS LIFE ON THE 18TH OF JULY 1817, AGED 41, AFTER A LONG ILLNESS SUPPORTED WITH THE PATIENCE AND THE HOPES OF A CHRISTIAN. THE BENEVOLENCE OF HER HEART, THE SWEETNESS OF HER TEMPER, AND THE EXTRAORDINARY ENDOWMENTS OF HER MIND OBTAINED THE REGARD OF ALL WHO KNEW HER AND THE WARMEST LOVE OF HER INTIMATE CONNECTIONS. THEIR GRIEF IS IN PROPORTION TO THEIR AFFECTION, THEY KNOW THEIR LOSS TO BE IRREPARABLE, BUT IN THEIR DEEPEST AFFLICTION THEY ARE CONSOLED BY A FIRM THOUGH HUMBLE HOPE THAT HER CHARITY, DEVOTION, FAITH AND PURITY HAVE RENDERED HER SOUL ACCEPTABLE IN THE SIGHT OF HER REDEEMER.

JANE AUSTEN

02
WORLD

"NONE OF US WANT TO BE IN

CALM WATERS ALL OUR LIVES."

—Jane Austen, *Persuasion*, 1817

THE WORLD AT WAR

Britain was at war for 22 of Jane Austen's 41 years, but most readers would spot only hints of the conflict in her work. France was the usual enemy – the Revolutionary and Napoleonic wars stretched with little intermission between 1793 and 1815. At various times Britain was also embroiled with Spain, Russia and Holland.

Two of Austen's brothers, Francis and Charles, were naval men, and she was knowledgeable about navy life. The dockyard scenes at Portsmouth in *Mansfield Park* and the various naval personalities in *Persuasion* demonstrate her familiarity. By contrast, she does not usually discuss the army in terms of career. Regiments in her lifetime were either militia – non-career soldiers conscripted as they were needed – or 'regular' – made up of men who had chosen the army as a career. The regiment billeted in Meryton in *Pride and Prejudice* is a militia regiment, and George Wickham is a militia officer; by contrast, Frederick Tilney, in *Northanger Abbey*, is a member of the regulars. Incidentally, both are arrant flirts, though only one is a villain.

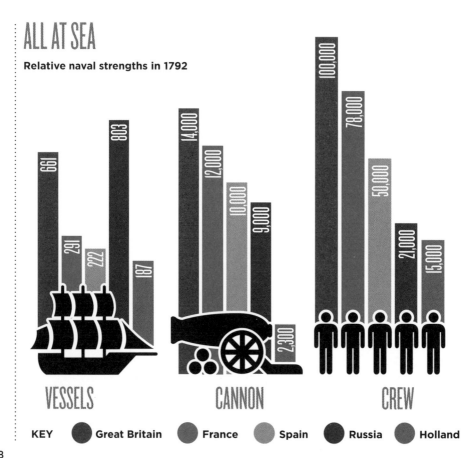

ALL AT SEA

Relative naval strengths in 1792

VESSELS: 669, 291, 222, 803, 187

CANNON: 14,000, 12,000, 10,000, 9,000, 2,300

CREW: 100,000, 78,000, 50,000, 21,000, 15,000

KEY — Great Britain · France · Spain · Russia · Holland

NUMBER OF MEN IN THE BRITISH ARMY:

1793	40,000
1813	250,000

AGE OF BRITISH INFANTRY DURING NAPOLEONIC WARS:

OVER 30 YEARS OLD | UNDER 18 | BETWEEN 18 AND 29

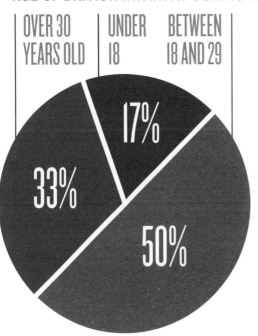

17%

33%

50%

In *Pride and Prejudice*, a red coat – disastrously – conquers all for the younger, sillier Bennet sisters. Salman Rushdie neatly summed it up:

"THE FUNCTION OF THE BRITISH ARMY IN THE NOVELS OF JANE AUSTEN IS TO LOOK CUTE AT PARTIES."

Teeth pulled from the bodies of dead soldiers were popular for British dentures. 'Waterloo teeth' were advertised as such because the teeth in them would be of the finest quality, having come from young, fit men.

IN POSSESSION OF A GOOD FORTUNE?

Elegantly inexplicit it may sometimes be, but Jane Austen's message to her heroines is very clear: it may be wicked to marry for money, but it is stupid to marry without it. The majority of her leading ladies, in particular the elder Bennet and Dashwood sisters of *Pride and Prejudice* and *Sense and Sensibility* respectively, are, in financial terms, Cinderella figures who marry 'up' and can look forward to a solvent future. Luckily, they tend to fall in love while doing so. Lesser characters may not always be granted the same good fortune, and sometimes their come-uppance is also part of the novel.

How much money each union involves in today's terms can be hard to make out. Two centuries ago, some items – food, clothing, transport – were much more expensive than today, but servants and labour were infinitely cheaper.

ANNUAL INCOMES 1800 – 1820

£15 – £25
Labourer
(might include a tied cottage if working on an estate)

£25
Governess
(would have food and lodging as part of the job)

£40
Curate
(would include accommodation)

£150
Gentleman of modest means

£500
Gentleman of moderate means

£1200
Well-to-do gentleman
(enough to maintain a carriage)

SENSE AND SENSIBILITY

Elinor Dashwood
marries
Edward Ferrars

£ £ £ £ £
Before:
family income of £500 pa, living with her mother and sisters.

£ £ £ £ £
After:
income of £850 pa when his mother relents after their marriage.

Marianne Dashwood
marries
Colonel Brandon

£ £ £ £ £
Before:
family income of £500 pa, living with her mother and sisters.

£ £ £ £ £
After:
income of £2,000 pa.

Across Austen's lifetime, any amount over £2,000 was a handsome annual income

PRIDE AND PREJUDICE

Elizabeth Bennet
marries
Fitzwilliam Darcy

Before:
£100 pa before her father's death; £1,000 lump sum after it.

After:
£10,000 pa, substantial assets, including an estate at Pemberley.

Jane Bennet
marries
Charles Bingley

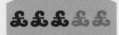

Before:
£100 pa before her father's death; £1,000 lump sum after it.

After:
£5,000 pa.

Lydia Bennet
marries
George Wickham

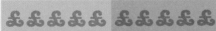

Before:
£100 pa before her father's death; £1,000 lump sum after it.

After:
income unknown; bribed to marry her by Darcy, his debts paid off, an ensigncy in the Army purchased, and possibly a lump sum.

NORTHANGER ABBEY

Catherine Morland
marries
Henry Tilney

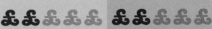

Before:
family income unknown; one of 10 children of a comfortable gentleman, so prospects limited, possibly c. £3,000.

After: rector of a parish; likely heir to some of his father's fortune, comfortably off; income unknown.

EMMA

Emma Woodhouse
marries
George Knightley

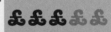

Before:
inheritance of £30,000.

After:
income unknown, gentleman, farmer, owner of Donwell Abbey, sizeable lands, carriage and horses.

Jane Fairfax
marries
Frank Churchill

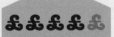

Before:
no income; dependent orphan; prospects as governess.

After:
income unknown, gentleman; substantial inheritance prospects from his rich aunt.

HAVING A BALL

The ball, whether held as a private party or a public event, features in every one of Jane Austen's novels. And this isn't surprising, as dancing was one of the main social pleasures of country and town life. Dancing was a way to meet new people, and the only chance young men and women might have for genteel physical contact with people they didn't know well: the first spark of romance was often ignited in a ballroom. Private balls were invitation-only, but anyone could buy a ticket to a public dance. Organizing timings for a ball out of town depended on a number of factors, not all of them obvious: full moon was a popular date for a private ball, as it ensured guests would have a well-lit road to go home by.

WHAT TO WEAR?

Ladies: their finest clothes and ornaments in pale colours, elaborately dressed hair with ornaments.

Gentlemen: knee breeches, from around 1810 usually in black, with matching black stockings.

ARRIVAL...
HOW TO GET THERE

You wouldn't have walked! You would have taken a carriage in the country or a carriage or sedan chair in town.

DANCING ...
WHICH DANCE?

- Each dance lasts around half an hour, and partners usually engage for a pair of dances.

- You can only dance with someone to whom you have been formally introduced.

- If you don't want to dance with a particular partner, the only workable excuses are tiredness or being previously engaged to another partner.

The waltz: introduced in high society from 1810 onwards, but didn't filter down to less sophisticated society for a few years.

The boulanger: a round dance, performed in a circle.

Country dances: danced in a long line of couples. Each couple dances their way from the bottom of the line to the top.

The cotillion: a square dance of four couples.

The minuet: old-fashioned by the 1800s, but still used as a way for one couple to open a ball.

SUPPER...
WHAT TO EAT?

Supper was presented as a sit-down buffet with various dishes.

Cold meats and pies

Hot 'ragouts' of veal or fowl

'White soup': contains almonds and chicken or veal stock

Cold fish

Jellies, ices, cream fools, sponge cakes and biscuits

To drink: wine, punch, or negus (hot, sugared, watered wine)

HOW LONG DOES A BALL LAST?

Usually, as long as the candles. Candles were made to last four or six hours, or even longer. Private houses might replace candles over a long evening; but in a public ballroom, dancing stopped when the candles burned down.

WHO DRIVES WHAT?

Looking at the fatiguing difficulties of transport in Regency times, it seems astonishing that people travelled as much as they did – Austen had an impressively busy schedule of visits to friends and relatives. Roads were often terrible; Mr Darcy's famous speech "and what is 50 miles of good road?" is the voice of privilege – he can afford all the horses and carriages he needs for the easiest possible journey. We can see from Austen's novels and letters that horses and carriages were discussed easily as much as cars are today. So which carriage was the people-carrier and which the sports car in Regency Britain?

COACH

The traditional closed vehicle; used in town to spare you some of the dirt and smells.

Kept by: the Bennets in *Pride and Prejudice*; the Musgroves in *Persuasion*

HORSES: 4–6 / PASSENGERS: 4–6

CHAISE

An enclosed vehicle, substantially smaller than a coach.

Kept by: Mr Bingley, Lady Catherine de Bourgh and Mr Gardiner in *Pride and Prejudice*; Mrs Jennings in *Sense and Sensibility*; Lady Bertram in *Mansfield Park*

HORSES: 2–4 / PASSENGERS: 3

CHARIOT

An enclosed vehicle with a coach box and a driver.

Kept by: Mrs Rushworth in *Mansfield Park*

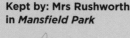

HORSES: 2–4 / PASSENGERS: 3

BAROUCHE

PEOPLE CARRIER!

A heavy, open four-wheeler, mostly for formal town use.

Kept by: Henry Crawford in *Mansfield Park*; Lady Dalrymple in *Persuasion*

HORSES: 4 / PASSENGERS: 5

LANDAU

A light four-wheeler with a soft top.

No Austen characters admit to owning a Landau

HORSES: 2–4 / PASSENGERS: 4

PHAETON

A popular light, low-sided four-wheeler for leisure driving.

Kept by Miss de Bourgh in *Pride and Prejudice*; Mrs Gardiner posits that Elizabeth will be wanting a phaeton after her marriage to Darcy

HORSES: 2 / PASSENGERS: 1

CURRICLE

A light, fast two-wheeled chariot for sport and leisure driving.

Kept by: John Willoughby in *Sense and Sensibility*; Henry Tilney in *Northanger Abbey*, Mr Darcy in *Pride and Prejudice*, Walter Elliot in *Persuasion*

HORSES: 1 / PASSENGERS: 1

LANDAULETTE

Vehicle of choice for fashionable ladies; easily driven and pulled by smaller horses or ponies.

Kept by: Anne Elliot, after her marriage, in *Persuasion*

HORSES: 2 / PASSENGERS: 2

GIG

A generic one-horse vehicle, light enough for women to drive and less expensive than a curricle.

Kept by: Admiral Croft in *Persuasion*, Mr Collins in *Pride and Prejudice*

HORSES: 1 / PASSENGERS: 1

WORLD

LUNCH IS FOR WIMPS

To the modern mind, who eats what and when can be confusing in the novels of Jane Austen. Above the working class, who fitted their meals around their labours and ate whatever they could afford, the middle and upper classes ate late – and the higher their social aspirations, the later the mealtimes. Breakfast might come after morning exercise, while dinner was served, at the earliest, mid-afternoon. 'Tea' might incorporate food as well, while supper in a fashionable household might be served very late indeed. Parson Woodforde, the Norfolk vicar who kept lively diaries from the mid-1770s until he died in 1803, provides a full account of his meals, which gives some idea of the sheer quantity of food on the late 18th-century table, even for those of comparatively modest means.

Breakfast was taken mid- to late morning, typically 10–11am (as late as noon for the fashionable).

BREAKFAST
10–11 AM

SUPPER
9–10 PM

9

Supper was taken in the late evening, typically 9–10pm (again, as late as midnight in fashionable circles).

TEA
6–7 PM

2

IN THE SUMMER OF 1784, PARSON WOODFORDE
HAD FRIENDS TO DINNER AND SERVED...

"some Pike,

a Couple
of Fowls
boiled

and Piggs
Face,

green Peas Soup

3

and a prodigious Fricasse,

Dinner was taken mid- to
late afternoon, typically
3–4pm (as late as 6 or
6.30pm in fashionable
circles, in which case tea
might not happen at all).

a Couple of Ducks
roasted, green Peas,

DINNER
3–4 PM

plumb Pudding,

Maccaroni
& c..."

Tea was taken in
the early evening,
typically 6–7pm.

Washed down with beer and port, with
brandy afterwards, this was a straightforward
meal for friends, rather than a notable feast.
Austen's gourmet clergyman Dr Grant, in *Mansfield
Park,* could clearly have been modelled from real life.

BESTSELLERS

From the perspective of the multi-million bestseller, the world of publishing in Jane Austen's time is almost unrecognizable. Four of her works were published – thanks largely to the efforts of her brother Henry – in her lifetime, but it was only with *Emma*, in 1815, that she engaged with the celebrity publisher of the day, John Murray.

Murray was unusual – the son of a publisher, also John Murray, he was more entrepreneurial than many of the combined booksellers/publishers of his day. It's unknown why he was prepared to take a punt on Jane Austen, whose books had sold well but not spectacularly for her previous publisher, Thomas Egerton, but William Gifford, editor of Murray's periodical, the *Quarterly Review*, is known to have recommended Austen to Murray in 1814. Jane herself corresponded with Murray in straightforward and businesslike terms.

What did it take to make a bestseller in the first decade or two of the 19th century?

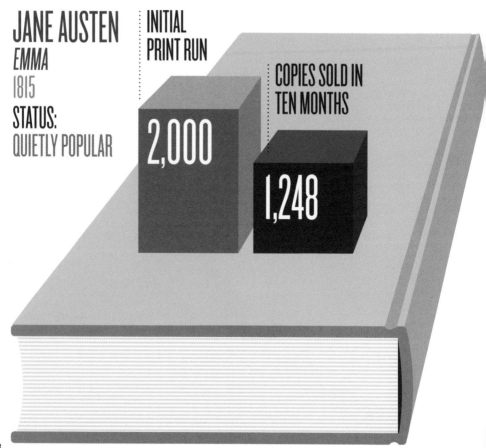

JANE AUSTEN
EMMA
1815
STATUS:
QUIETLY POPULAR

INITIAL PRINT RUN

2,000

COPIES SOLD IN TEN MONTHS

1,248

LORD BYRON
CHILDE HAROLD'S PILGRIMAGE
1812
STATUS:
BOTH THE BOOK AND ITS ARISTOCRATIC 24-YEAR-OLD AUTHOR BECAME LONDON SENSATIONS

While Byron "awoke and found myself famous", Austen's gift would take longer to gain recognition and Jane wasn't immune to author's pre-publication jitters:

"I AM VERY STRONGLY HAUNTED BY THE IDEA THAT TO THOSE READERS WHO HAVE PREFERRED P&P [PRIDE AND PREJUDICE] IT WILL APPEAR INFERIOR IN WIT, & TO THOSE WHO HAVE PREFERRED MP [*MANSFIELD PARK*] VERY INFERIOR IN GOOD SENSE."

—From a letter to John Murray, 11 December 1815

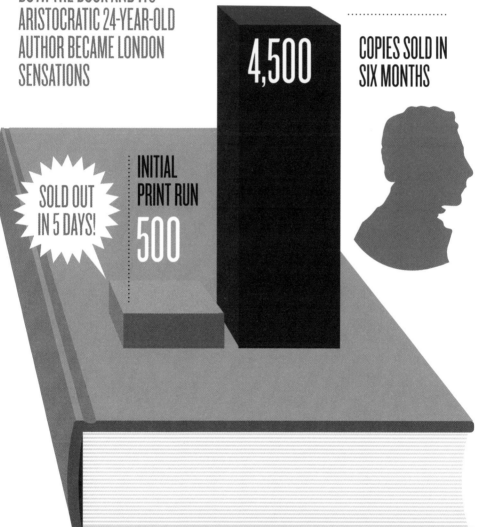

4,500 COPIES SOLD IN SIX MONTHS

SOLD OUT IN 5 DAYS!

INITIAL PRINT RUN **500**

QUADRILLE

A formal game of skill

SPECULATION

A simple gambling game

+

That Lady Bertram in *Mansfield Park* finds it so challenging is an indication of her stupidity.

 Difficulty

 Number of players

A GAME OF CARDS

Almost all Jane Austen's characters play cards; the card table in a late 18th- or early 19th-century evening's diversion was as ubiquitous as a television set would be today. Preferences for different games could hint at character, but domestic games were often played for fun not money. In *Pride and Prejudice*, frequent mention is made of evenings at cards (Lydia, characteristically, loves Lottery Tickets, while the fashionable circle at Netherfield play Loo). However, this isn't seen as gambling, just harmless entertainment. When Wickham is revealed as a hardened gambler and ne'er-do-well, on the other hand, Jane Bennet is shocked: "A gamester!... This is wholly unexpected. I had not an idea of it."

The 'fish' often mentioned as the fruits of domestic card games in Austen's novels are mother-of-pearl counters, like poker chips today; they were imported from China and were often fish-shaped.

LOO

A round game with many variations

WHIST

Similar to bridge, played in teams

+

PIQUET

A classic card game of skill

LOTTERY TICKETS

A game of pure chance

03
WORK

"THAT YOUNG LADY HAD A TALENT FOR DESCRIBING... ORDINARY LIFE WHICH IS TO ME THE MOST WONDERFUL I EVER MET WITH. THE BIG BOW-WOW STRAIN I CAN DO MYSELF... BUT THE EXQUISITE TOUCH WHICH RENDERS... ORDINARY, COMMONPLACE THINGS AND CHARACTERS INTERESTING... IS DENIED TO ME."

—Sir Walter Scott, in his journal, 14 March 1826

LOCATION, LOCATION, LOCATION

Apart from a very few glancing references (as when Julia Bertram is suddenly "gone to Scotland with Yates" at the denouement of *Mansfield Park*), Austen's novels are firmly located in relatively small areas of south/south-west England. The ladies and gentlemen who populate them are the polar opposite of the heroes and heroines of her contemporaries' Gothic novels, who are invariably carried off to dramatically described but ill-defined destinations – Sicily, perhaps, or the Alps. Austen stuck to what she knew, not only in her social circle but in the landscapes that surrounded her characters, too, venturing north only as far as Derbyshire (in *Pride and Prejudice*). This map shows how the fictional locations in all six novels fit in with real ones.

KEY

Fictional locations

Sense and Sensiblity

Pride and Prejudice

Northanger Abbey

Mansfield Park

Emma

Persuasion

Real locations featured in Jane Austen's books

South Park

Maple Grove

Bristol

Bath

Thornberry Park

Winthrop

Kellynch Hall, Uppercross, Monkford

Allenham, Barton Park, Newton

Exeter

DEVON

Whitwell

CORNWALL

Longstaple

Plymouth

Pemberley

DERBYSHIRE

Everingham

Sotherton

Lessingby

Mansfield Park

NORFOLK

Thornton Lacey

Meryton, Longbourn

Northanger
Abbey

Brockham

Netherfield Park

NORTHAMPTONSHIRE   CAMBRIDGESHIRE

SUFFOLK

WARWICKSHIRE

Hatfield

London

Blenheim

ESSEX

Oxford

GLOUCESTERSHIRE   OXFORDSHIRE

HERTFORDSHIRE

Bromley

Woodston

Windsor

Westerham

MIDDLESEX

BERKSHIRE

WILTSHIRE

SURREY

KENT

Cleveland

Marlborough

Hunsford

Combe Magna

Fullerton

Rosings Park

HAMPSHIRE

SUSSEX

DORSET

Highbury,
Hartfield,
Donwell Abbey

Dartford

Delaford

Brighton

Weymouth

Isle of Wight

Norland Park

A LATE BLOOMER

Jane Austen wrote from childhood but her first novel wasn't published until she was 35. Very few authors are lucky enough, like Byron, to "awake and find [themselves] famous". Far more serve a long, hard apprenticeship, and Austen was not initially lucky with her publishers. Her father made the first attempt to have one of her books – *First Impressions* (which would become *Pride and Prejudice*) –

published by Thomas Cadell, who published the novels of Fanny Burney, but his offer was rejected by return of post, while another publisher, Benjamin Crosby, accepted *Susan* (later to become *Northanger Abbey*) but then sat on it without publishing for years, until Austen could finally afford to buy back the rights a year before she died.

How does Austen measure up against other authors? Here's how old a selection of greats were when they broke through, and the work – not always their first – that did the trick. As the line-up shows, Austen was far from unusual in having had to wait until her mid-30s to see her first novel in print, and successfully so.

20	23	24	24	24	25	25	26	29	31
Mary Shelley *Frankenstein*	F Scott Fitzgerald *This Side of Paradise*	Alexander Pope *The Rape of the Lock*	Lord Byron *Childe Harold's Pilgrimage*	Charles Dickens *The Pickwick Papers*	Fyodor Dostoyevsky *Poor Folk*	Evelyn Waugh *Decline and Fall*	William Shakespeare *Henry VI, part 2*	Emily Brontë *Wuthering Heights*	Charlotte Brontë *Jane Eyre*

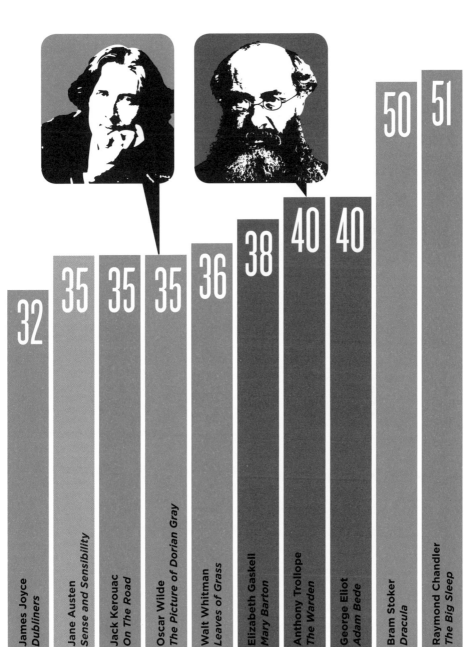

32

35

35

35

36

38

40

40

50

51

James Joyce
Dubliners

Jane Austen
Sense and Sensibility

Jack Kerouac
On The Road

Oscar Wilde
The Picture of Dorian Gray

Walt Whitman
Leaves of Grass

Elizabeth Gaskell
Mary Barton

Anthony Trollope
The Warden

George Eliot
Adam Bede

Bram Stoker
Dracula

Raymond Chandler
The Big Sleep

WORK

SEALED WITH A KISS

How many kisses are written into Austen's novels? Those who see Austen as one of the great romantics have often tried to count them. Yet all have concluded that there are no kisses between lovers in any of the books. There are some near misses, but the kisses actually noted are variously indicators of sibling affection, respect between friends or marks of gratitude. Here's the tally (discounting a few given to children) along with some charged moments that undoubtedly mean as much, if not more, than any mere kiss could.

KISS-O-METER

♥ LOVER'S KISS

✗ FRIENDLY KISS

✗ FAMILY KISS

SENSE AND SENSIBILITY

 Willoughby kisses the lock of hair that Marianne has given him

 Elinor kisses Marianne to comfort her after Willoughby denies their relationship

 Colonel Brandon kisses Elinor's hand after she has listened to his account of Willoughby's iniquity

 Marianne kisses Elinor to thank her for her support

PRIDE AND PREJUDICE

 Mr Wickham ruefully kisses Elizabeth's hand after she reveals that she knows his full history ("though he hardly knew where to look")

 Jane kisses her father when he congratulates her on her engagement to Mr Bingley

 CHARGED MOMENT:

Charlotte Collins notices that Mr Darcy cannot stop looking at Elizabeth whenever they are in the same room.

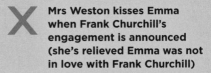

EMMA

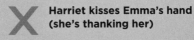

X Harriet kisses Emma's hand (she's thanking her)

X Mrs Weston kisses Emma when Frank Churchill's engagement is announced (she's relieved Emma was not in love with Frank Churchill)

 CHARGED MOMENT:

Shortly before Mr Knightley declares for Emma, he takes her hand, but shakes it instead of kissing it. For Emma, it's the start of her conscious physical awareness of him.

MANSFIELD PARK

X Sir Thomas Bertram kisses Fanny

X William Price kisses Fanny twice

X Fanny kisses Sir Thomas Bertram's hand (she's displeased him)

X Mrs Price kisses Fanny

X Fanny kisses Tom and Charles Price (her brothers)

CHARGED MOMENT:

Henry Crawford and Maria Bertram, trying not to embrace while rehearsing *Lovers' Vows*.

NORTHANGER ABBEY AND PERSUASION

Neither *Northanger Abbey* nor *Persuasion* have any recorded kisses, unless you count – in the latter – the elderly Sir Archibald Drew kissing his hand to Anne in salutation as he drives past.

 CHARGED MOMENT:

Persuasion, however, has possibly the most passionate section in any of Austen's work: Captain Wentworth's yearning love letter to Anne.

WORK

HOLY ORDERS

Jane Austen knew a good deal about life in the Church – not only was her father a parson, but so, too, was one of her brothers, James. Her favourite brother, Henry, was also a clergyman in his wide selection of careers. And in her day, a profession is exactly what the Church was – it wasn't considered necessary for a man to have a particular calling to join the Church, and it was a popular choice for the younger sons of the landed gentry, particularly if their parents could provide them with a parish or 'living'. Richer clergymen might preside over two or three parishes, from which they might take quite a good income in the form of tithes.

In her six novels, Jane Austen features 12 clergymen – including those who aren't quite ordained yet, like Edmund Bertram in *Mansfield Park* or Charles Hayter, who is curate to Dr Shirley in *Persuasion*. She ensures that they are as various as any other cross-section of society, from the vain, socially ambitious Mr Elton and the gourmand Dr Grant to the intelligent Henry Tilney and Mr Collins, surely one of the most enjoyably ghastly characters ever invented.

Clergymen and their novels:

Sense and Sensibility
Edward Ferrars

Pride and Prejudice
Mr Collins

Northanger Abbey
Henry Tilney, Mr Morland,
James Morland

Mansfield Park
Edmund Bertram, Mr Norris,
Dr Grant

Emma
Mr Elton *(below in vicar's outfit of the time)*, Charles Hayter

Persuasion
Dr Shirley, Mr Wentworth

Unless he was from a rich family, the vicar's lot was not necessarily a financially easy one – and the position was even trickier for his dependent curate.

£100 – £1,000

Range of annual income that might be provided by a parish.

£50

Minimum annual salary supposed to be paid to a curate by a vicar, but many received much less than this.

3,000

Parishes in England that did not provide clergymen with living quarters at the beginning of the 19th century.

50%

The proportion of parishes in England that were in the gift of private landlords at the beginning of the 19th century.

2,000

Number of England's parishes that had a rectory unfit to live in at the beginning of the 19th century.

Prejudiced by the habits of Dr Grant, her lazy, greedy brother-in-law, the sparkling Mary Crawford makes a scathing dismissal of clergymen in *Mansfield Park*:

"A CLERGYMAN HAS NOTHING TO DO BUT BE SLOVENLY AND SELFISH – READ THE NEWSPAPER, WATCH THE WEATHER, AND QUARREL WITH HIS WIFE. HIS CURATE DOES ALL THE WORK, AND THE BUSINESS OF HIS OWN LIFE IS TO DINE."

She is shooting herself in the foot, because Edmund Bertram, with whom she is fast falling in love, is shortly to be ordained.

WORK

"HORRID NOVELS"

When Jane Austen satirized the craze for Gothic novels in *Northanger Abbey*, she knew what she was talking about. Novels weren't held in great regard by the high-minded or the consciously informed, but they were extremely popular. In the early 19th century, most would have been obtained from the circulating libraries (a new novel, usually served up in three volumes, would cost the equivalent of three or four days' wages for a skilled worker, but you could join a library and take two volumes out at a time for an annual fee of around 2 guineas, a substantial saving). In 1801, there were around 1,000 such libraries in Britain – and you went there, not only to get your new books, but also to be seen: they were fashionable places to visit.

10 real-life novels featured in *Northanger Abbey*:

THE CASTLE OF WOLFENBACH — ELIZA PARSONS — 1793

THE NECROMANCER — LUDWIG FLAMMENBERG — 1794

THE MYSTERIES OF UDOLPHO — ANN RADCLIFFE

THE MONK: A ROMANCE — MATTHEW LEWIS — 1796

THE HORRID MYSTERIES, A STORY FROM THE GERMAN OF THE MARQUIS OF GROSSE — CARL GROSSE

GOTHIC INGREDIENTS

The gasped-over *The Mysteries of Udolpho* has plenty of 'horrid' Gothic ingredients, listed here. Wrapped up in four volumes, it is a lengthy and (by modern standards) turgid read.

 1 x 'sensible' – that is, hysterical – heroine, Emily St Aubert

 1 x mysterious black veil

 1 x gloomy castle (Udolpho)

1 x enforced visit to Venice

 1 x accidental shooting, of Valancourt, her suitor

 1 x nun with a secret identity

 1 x wax model of a decayed corpse

 1 x bandit hideout in the mountains

THE MYSTERIOUS WARNING: A GERMAN TALE — ELIZA PARSONS

THE ITALIAN — ANN RADCLIFFE

CLERMONT: A TALE — REGINA MARIA ROCHE

THE MIDNIGHT BELL: A GERMAN STORY, FOUNDED ON INCIDENTS IN REAL LIFE — HD SYMONDS

THE ORPHAN OF THE RHINE: A ROMANCE — ELEANOR SLEATH

1797

1798

IN FRONT OF THE SERVANTS

Servants don't get many speeches in the works of Jane Austen, but they're nearly always there, often in number. Named or not, they have many roles to play. They may prevent the protagonists acting on their wishes (*Emma*, for example, has to wait until her hair is curled and the maid has been sent away "to be miserable" about her muddle with Mr Elton); offer a commentary on events (in *Mansfield Park*, we get a feeling of the sheer scale of the household when we learn that the scene painter for the amateur theatricals has rendered "five of the under-servants idle and dissatisfied"), or express the standing of the household in

STEWARD (only in the grandest households, ranked over butler and housekeeper)

HOUSEKEEPER

BUTLER

GAMEKEEPER

COOK

LADY'S MAID

HEAD NURSE

LAUNDRY MAID/S

GARDENER

KITCHEN MAID/S

HOUSEMAID/S

(if there are children)

NURSERY MAID/S

general (like the slatternly Rebecca, also in *Mansfield Park*, who is one of only two servants in the poor Price household in Portsmouth).

They can propel scandal too – Lydia Bennet's elopement and Maria Rushworth's disgrace are the subject of servants' gossip in the first case and – worse – actual blackmail in the second.

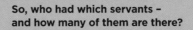

So, who had which servants – and how many of them are there?

EMMA
Cook Serle, at Hartfield
Coachman James, at Hartfield
Housekeeper Mrs Hodges, at Donwell Abbey
Maid of all work Patty, at Mrs and Miss Bates' house

MANSFIELD PARK
Housekeeper Mrs Whitaker, at Sotherton
Butler Baddeley, at Mansfield Park
Coachman Wilcox, at Mansfield Park
Lady's maid Chapman, at Mansfield Park
Maid of all work Rebecca, at the Price's house in Portsmouth

PRIDE AND PREJUDICE
Housekeeper Mrs Hill, at Longbourn
Housekeeper Mrs Reynolds, at Pemberley

PERSUASION
Nursery-maid Jemima, at Uppercross
Gardener Mackenzie, at Kellynch

VALET   COACHMAN

FOOTMEN   GROOMS

SCULLION/ KITCHEN BOY   BAILIFF

SERVANTS OF THE POOR

If you were born into the middle classes, you had to fall very far indeed not to have servants. Even the needy Mrs and Miss Bates in *Emma* have Patty, an all-purpose maid. Mrs Dashwood, fallen to a situation of genteel economy in *Sense and Sensibility*, still employs two maids and a manservant. Only once, in *Persuasion*, do we hear of a lady too poor to employ any sort of servant.

and finally, in an awkward position, off to the side, neither quite staff nor quite family...

THE GOVERNESS

WORK

"ANOTHER STUPID PARTY LAST NIGHT..."

It is well recorded that Jane Austen had mixed feelings about Bath – family legend held that she fainted when told of the move, and her letters to Cassandra are full of her hatred of "stupid parties". She lived there for nearly five years, based first at 4 Sydney Place, moving to Green Park Buildings in 1804, and briefly at 25 Gay Street before finally departing Bath in 1806. It was a fallow time for writing, but both *Northanger Abbey* and *Persuasion* make heavy use of Bath – the first views it through the eyes of Catherine Morland, with enthusiastic innocence, the second sees the city through the sadder, more jaded eyes of Anne Elliot.

25 Gay Street (1805–06)
The family moves closer to Jane's uncle before leaving Bath for good.

13 Queen's Square (1799)
A little over a month's stay during the summer.

3 Green Park (1804–05)
The death of George Austen forced the family to move.

WHY NOT BATH?

Anne Elliot's family discuss three options: London, Bath or another house in the country:

"ALL ANNE'S WISHES HAD BEEN FOR THE LATTER. SHE DISLIKED BATH, AND DID NOT THINK IT AGREED WITH HER – AND BATH WAS TO BE HER HOME."

HUSBAND HUNTING?

Claire Tomalin, Austen's biographer, suggests that Jane disliked Bath because she suspected that the reason her parents had moved was so that she and Cassandra might find husbands. A vain hope, if so.

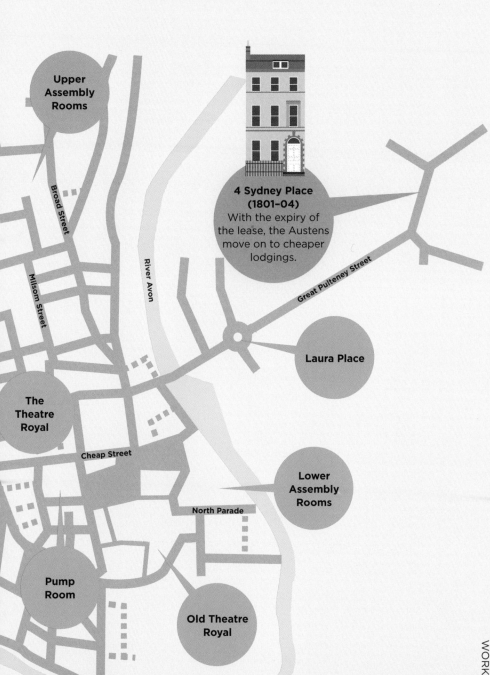

Upper Assembly Rooms

Broad Street

Milsom Street

River Avon

4 Sydney Place (1801–04)
With the expiry of the lease, the Austens move on to cheaper lodgings.

Great Pulteney Street

Laura Place

The Theatre Royal

Cheap Street

Lower Assembly Rooms

North Parade

Pump Room

Old Theatre Royal

FIRST DRAFT
CHAPTER 10/11

18 July 1816

Persuasion tells the story of a second chance at lost love. Navy Captain Frederick Wentworth (CW) and Anne Elliot (AE), previously engaged, meet again after no contact in more than seven years

18 July–6 August 1816

SECOND DRAFT
CHAPTER 10/11

Emotional reaction

CW's sister and her husband plot to place the couple in a room together

CW and AE reconcile their love naturally upon seeing each other

HOW ARE THEY RECONCILED?

REKINDLED ROMANCE

CW overhears AE discussing the topic of love; stirs emotions in CW

Anne acts as if "persuaded" by CW, in reality never stopped loving him

CW writes a letter to AE declaring his love for her

PLOTS OF *PERSUASION*

Persuasion has been lauded as Austen's most poignant novel: the love story of Anne Elliot (who, at the age of just 28, has lost the bloom of youth) and Frederick Wentworth who was judged, a decade previously, not eligible enough to marry

her. It's also the only one of Austen's books for which a portion of the original manuscript survives. The original final chapters, 10 and 11, are now in the British Library, and they contain a different ending from that in the published book.

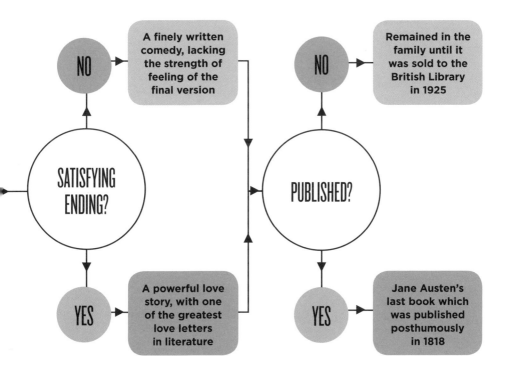

NO → A finely written comedy, lacking the strength of feeling of the final version

SATISFYING ENDING?

YES → A powerful love story, with one of the greatest love letters in literature

NO → Remained in the family until it was sold to the British Library in 1925

PUBLISHED?

YES → Jane Austen's last book which was published posthumously in 1818

"I CAN LISTEN NO LONGER IN SILENCE. I MUST SPEAK TO YOU BY SUCH MEANS AS ARE WITHIN MY REACH. YOU PIERCE MY SOUL. I AM HALF AGONY, HALF HOPE... DARE NOT SAY THAT MAN FORGETS SOONER THAN WOMAN, THAT HIS LOVE HAS AN EARLIER DEATH. I HAVE LOVED NONE BUT YOU."

WORK

JANE AUSTEN 1775–1817

Fanny Burney was one of the most popular novelists of the 1770s and '80s but sadly today few readers could name the four novels that made her famous. The life she led was very different from Austen's. She was Keeper of the Robes to Queen Charlotte from 1786, and lived at court for some years; she married late, aged 41, to a French émigré. Their experiences of publishing were different, too, with Burney earning far more from her books in her lifetime than Austen ever did.

Style
It is hard for us to see at a distance of two centuries just how much of an innovator Jane Austen was. A keen and omnivorous reader herself, she was sharply aware of fresh trends as they arose (and was herself an admirer of Burney's work). The naturalistic dialogue and relatively unsensational nature of her novels both broke new ground for their time.

£790
Profits at time of death

6
Novels written

LOVE
Never married

Family
Daughter of clergyman, George Austen. She was one of eight children. She had six brothers and one sister.

1752–1840 FANNY BURNEY

Style
Although Burney's first novel, *Evelina*, was in epistolary form – written as a sequence of letters – as was fashionable in the mid-18th century, her three later works, *Cecilia* (1782), *Camilla* (1796) and *The Wanderer* (1814), were all third-person narratives. After her previous successes, her publisher paid an immense advance for *The Wanderer*. Unfortunately, by the time of its publication, her style was beginning to seem dated and it did not perform as well as was expected.

4
Novels written (as well as 8 plays, 20 volumes of journals and a biography)

LOVE
Married a French exile, General Alexandre D'Arblay. They had one son, Alexander

£4,280
Minimum profits at time of death

Family
Daughter of the music historian and composer, Dr Charles Burney. She was one of six children. She had three sisters and two brothers.

LADY OF LETTERS

Based on a complicated sum involving the people she usually wrote to, the amount of time she spent away from home, the amount of time that Regency ladies usually spent on correspondence... and so on... it has been estimated that Jane Austen probably wrote around 3,000 letters in the course of her short life. Sadly, few survive – Cassandra Austen destroyed a great number after Jane's death, and excised passages from some of the remainder. Janeites are sometimes disappointed by the everyday tone of most of the letters; they are certainly not 'literary', but they don't lack in personality and can be bracingly sharp.

FOLDING LETTERS

Paper was expensive and envelopes were not in common use; most letters were written then folded in on themselves and sealed. Money might be added under the seal to cover the price of the postage.

💬 GOSSIP

"...She appeared exactly as she did in September, with the same broad face, diamond bandeau, white shoes, pink husband, & fat neck..." (Reporting after a ball)

—To Cassandra, 20 November 1800

FASHION

"I cannot help thinking that it is more natural to have flowers grow out of the head than fruit" (On trimming hats)

—To Cassandra, 11 June 1799

BUSINESS

"I must request the favour of you to call on me... A short conversation may perhaps do more than much writing" (Negotiating with the publisher)

—To John Murray, 3 November 1815

▥ NEWS

"How horrible it is to have so many people killed! And what a blessing that one cares for none of them" (On casualties of the Peninsular War)

—To Cassandra, 31 May 1811

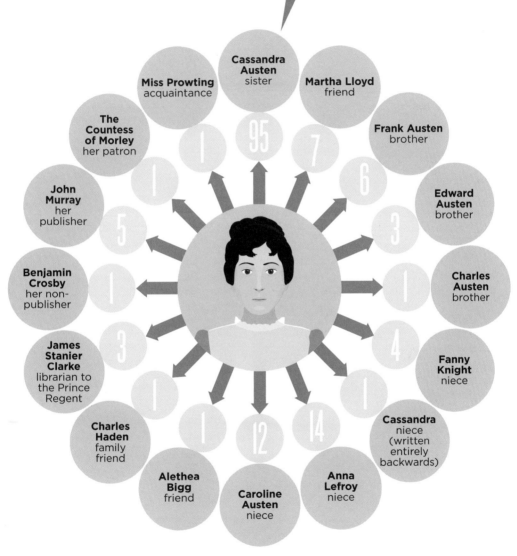

3,000 LETTERS JANE WROTE (APPROXIMATELY)

160 LETTERS THOUGHT TO HAVE SURVIVED

Cassandra Austen sister — 95

Miss Prowting acquaintance — 1

Martha Lloyd friend — 7

The Countess of Morley her patron — 1

Frank Austen brother — 6

John Murray her publisher — 5

Edward Austen brother — 3

Benjamin Crosby her non-publisher — 1

Charles Austen brother — 1

James Stanier Clarke librarian to the Prince Regent — 3

Fanny Knight niece — 4

Charles Haden family friend — 1

Cassandra niece (written entirely backwards) — 1

Alethea Bigg friend — 1

Caroline Austen niece — 12

Anna Lefroy niece — 14

+ A HANDFUL OF LETTERS EXIST FOR WHICH THE ADDRESSEES ARE UNKNOWN

THE PRESENCE OF PUG

Animals aren't much characterized by Jane Austen. Horses are used to get around on, and as signifiers of degrees of wealth, and a strong involvement with horse and hound is sometimes used to mark a young man of sporting interests. But there is only one true pet in her novels: Pug.

The familiar of the selfish, indolent Lady Bertram in *Mansfield Park*, Pug somehow manages to make his presence felt without getting a huge number of mentions.

5 FACTS ABOUT PUG

1 Pug is important to Lady Bertram: only half ironically, Austen tells us that she thinks more of him than of her children.

2 Like Lady Bertram, Pug usually spends his days on the sofa.

3 Pug occasionally gets active: after a hot day in the rose garden, Lady Bertram is exhausted by calling to keep him off the flower beds.

4 Pugs were fashionable throughout the 18th and 19th centuries: one appears in a portrait of Louis XIV; Goya painted the aristocratic Marquesa de Pontejos with her pug; and Hogarth's self-portrait included his pet.

5 Pug has progeny. When Fanny is courted by Henry Crawford, Lady Bertram shows her approval: "And I will tell you what, Fanny, which is more than I did for Maria: the next time Pug has a litter you shall have a puppy."

JANE
AUSTEN

04
LEGACY

"...OF ALL GREAT WRITERS SHE IS THE MOST DIFFICULT TO CATCH IN THE ACT OF GREATNESS..."

—Virginia Woolf, reviewing a new edition
of the complete novels, 30 January 1924

FROM LOCAL AUTHOR TO NATIONAL TREASURE

Just a few years after her death, Jane Austen's work had become – almost – obscure. The second edition of *Mansfield Park* sold poorly, and in 1821 John Murray remaindered *Northanger Abbey* and *Persuasion*, while Thomas Egerton, the publisher of *Pride and Prejudice* and *Sense and Sensibility*, seems to have remaindered his stock of both in 1817.

Recovery was slow, but a memoir published in 1870, combined with gradual but increasing critical recognition, was eventually to turn the molehill of Austen's reputation into a mountain. By the 1930s, she was a national treasure; by the 1990s, critical favour and a near-constant movie and television presence had turned her into an acknowledged literary giant.

1821

Richard Whately, Archbishop of Dublin, publishes an extended piece on Austen in the *Quarterly Review*, praising her work as being in the vanguard of the new style of realism in novels.

1870

James Edward Austen-Leigh publishes a memoir of his late aunt; fronted with an engraved portrait, it sells well, reviving public interest in Jane's novels.

1882

Richard Bentley publishes a collected edition of the novels known as 'The Steventon Edition', with more expensive binding and paper.

1832

Publisher Richard Bentley approaches the Austen family and buys the copyright to all the novels except *Pride and Prejudice* for £210. He acquires *Pride and Prejudice* from Thomas Egerton for £40, and issues all six in his small-format 'Standard Novels' series.

1860

The last of the copyrights on Austen's six novels expires. Bentley prints up to 1,000 copies of each title every 10 years – keeping them available, just.

1885

An entry for Jane Austen, written by Leslie Stephen (father of Virginia Woolf), appears in the *Dictionary of National Biography*.

JANE AUSTEN
LIVED HERE FROM 1809-1817
AND HENCE ALL HER WORKS
WERE SENT INTO THE WORLD
HER ADMIRERS IN THIS COUNTRY
AND IN AMERICA HAVE UNITED
TO ERECT THIS TABLET

SUCH ART AS HERS
CAN NEVER GROW OLD

1923
Robert Chapman's scholarly five-volume edition of Austen is published.

1933
The manuscript of *Lady Susan* is sold for £2,100 (then $8,812) to Walter M Hill, a bookseller from Chicago, at a Sotheby's sale.

1917
A plaque to commemorate Austen goes up on the wall of the cottage at Chawton.

1940
The psychologist and critic DW Harding publishes the essay 'Regulated Hatred', which makes a serious argument against the ruling 'cosy' image of Austen's work.

1940
Pride and Prejudice appears for the first time on the big screen, starring Greer Garson and Laurence Olivier. Aldous Huxley works on the screenplay.

1898
Félix Fénéon, author and anarchist, makes a 'literary' Austen translation. *Northanger Abbey* becomes *Catherine Morland* and is serialized in the *Revue Blanche*.

1940
Enthusiast Dorothy Darnell founds the Jane Austen Society of the UK, with the aim of fundraising to buy Chawton Cottage and create a museum there.

1978
Lord David Cecil's biography, *A Portrait of Jane Austen*, is published and proves popular.

1885
Allen & Macmillan publish a popular edition of *Pride and Prejudice* with 160 pictures by Hugh Thomson, a successful illustrator. They quickly come to epitomize Austen's public 'style'.

1979
The Jane Austen Society of North America is founded.

THE GOOD...

In the almost universal atmosphere of warm approval – from both everyday readers and literary critics – that surrounds Austen's art today, it can be hard to remember that some have actively disliked her novels. For Mark Twain, his loathing of her work became a literary joke, returned to at every conceivable opportunity ("once you put [one of her novels] down you simply can't pick it up") but before she became a household name, some people found fault quite innocently, unaware that they were criticizing a literary titan.

"ALSO READ AGAIN, AND FOR THE THIRD TIME AT LEAST, MISS AUSTEN'S VERY FINELY WRITTEN NOVEL OF *PRIDE AND PREJUDICE*. THAT YOUNG LADY HAD A TALENT FOR DESCRIBING THE INVOLVEMENTS AND FEELINGS AND CHARACTERS OF ORDINARY LIFE, WHICH IS TO ME THE MOST WONDERFUL I EVER MET WITH... WHAT A PITY SUCH A GIFTED CREATURE DIED SO EARLY."

—Sir Walter Scott, journal entry, 14 March 1826

"THE REALISM AND LIFE-LIKENESS OF MISS AUSTEN'S DRAMATIC PERSONAE COME NEAREST TO THOSE OF SHAKESPEARE. SHAKESPEARE HOWEVER IS A SUN TO WHICH JANE AUSTEN, THO' A BRIGHT AND TRUE LITTLE WORLD, IS BUT AN ASTEROID."

—Alfred, Lord Tennyson, quoted by his son Hallam, 1897

"ALL THE JANE AUSTEN CHARACTERS ARE READY FOR AN EXTENDED LIFE WHICH THE SCHEME OF HER BOOKS SELDOM REQUIRES THEM TO LEAD, AND THAT IS WHY THEY LEAD THEIR ACTUAL LIVES SO SATISFACTORILY... HOW JANE AUSTEN CAN WRITE!"

—EM Forster, *Aspects of the Novel*, 1927

THE BAD...

"I AM AT A LOSS TO UNDERSTAND WHY PEOPLE HOLD MISS AUSTEN'S NOVELS AT SO HIGH A RATE, WHICH SEEMS TO ME VULGAR IN TONE, STERILE IN ARTISTIC INVENTION, IMPRISONED IN THEIR WRETCHED CONVENTIONS OF ENGLISH SOCIETY, WITHOUT GENIUS, WIT OR KNOWLEDGE OF THE WORLD. NEVER WAS LIFE SO PINCHED AND SO NARROW... SUICIDE IS MORE RESPECTABLE."

—Ralph Waldo Emerson, notebooks, 1861

"THERE IS NO STORY IN IT, EXCEPT [THAT] SMOOTH, THIN WATER-GRUEL IS ACCORDING TO *EMMA'S* FATHER'S OPINION A VERY GOOD THING & IT IS VERY DIFFICULT TO MAKE A COOK UNDERSTAND WHAT YOU MEAN BY SMOOTH, THIN WATER-GRUEL."

—The novelist Maria Edgeworth, with her own tendencies to the Gothic, found *Emma* sadly undramatic.

AND THE UGLY!

"I HAVE TO STOP EVERY TIME I BEGIN. EVERY TIME I READ *PRIDE AND PREJUDICE* I WANT TO DIG HER UP AND BEAT HER OVER THE SKULL WITH HER OWN SHINBONE."

—Mark Twain, in a letter to his friend the Reverend Joseph Twichell, 1898

JANE AUSTEN'S HOUSE MUSEUM

Jane Austen's House Museum is located in the house at Chawton (Chawton Cottage, although to modern eyes it makes quite a grand cottage) near Alton in Hampshire where Austen lived with her mother and sister between 1809 and 1817. Bought in 1947 by TE Carpenter, and presented to the nation in memory of his son, who died in World War II, in 1949, the house has undergone many changes since Austen's day, having been converted into labourers' dwellings after Cassandra Austen's death in 1845. Nonetheless, it offers an atmospheric glimpse of country life lived in the early 19th century, and offers plenty of ephemera and mementoes to interest the Austen enthusiast.

THE AUSTENS' PATCHWORK QUILT

Worked by Jane, Cassandra and Mrs Austen. Features 64 chintz patterns.

"HAVE YOU REMEMBERED TO COLLECT PIECES FOR THE PATCHWORK? WE ARE NOW AT A STANDSTILL."

—Jane, in a letter to Cassandra Austen, May 1811

THE SPOILS OF WAR

The modest cache of jewellery on display at the museum includes the topaz crosses given to Jane and Cassandra by their sailor brother, Charles, in 1801 when he was rewarded for his part in the capture of a privateer. They are slightly different – Jane's is the one with the oval stones – and the gift may well have been the inspiration for the subplot involving an amber cross in _Mansfield Park_.

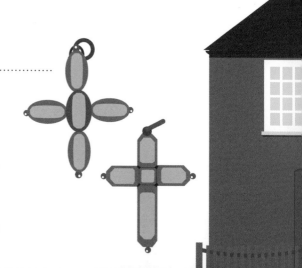

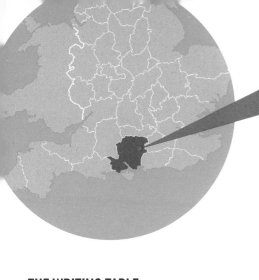

THE JANE AUSTEN'S HOUSE MUSEUM CHAWTON, ALTON, HAMPSHIRE

THE WRITING TABLE

The table at which Jane Austen wrote and revised on tiny handmade 'books' of folded paper is made from walnut, with a 12-sided top on a single tripod stand.

AUSTEN ON FILM

Even a casual headcount reveals well over 30 Austen movies, from straight filming of the novels to some much odder fare. Here's a headcount of some of the best or most interesting, with notes on what makes them stand out. Perhaps predictably, *Pride and Prejudice* tends to come out head and shoulders above the others, while some of the other novels seem to resist adaptation.

01 *Pride and Prejudice* (adaptation)
Robert Z Leonard, 1940

The first. Greer Garson pirouettes in vast taffeta gowns, while Laurence Olivier does his best romantic glowering. Aldous Huxley wrote some of the screenplay, which doesn't help much. Remarkable for the archery scene.

02 *Pride and Prejudice* (adaptation)
Simon Langton, 1995

Not technically a movie, but the mini-series ensures that the full plot can be given free rein, and the gratuitous Darcy-swimming scene, while not very Austen, charmed viewers. Perhaps one of the best Darcy/Elizabeth castings, in Colin Firth and Jennifer Ehle.

1940 Oscar for best art direction

05 *Mansfield Park* (adaptation)
Patricia Rozema, 1999

A ground-breaking interpretation featuring a sexually and socially-aware Fanny Price forging her own career as a writer.

06 *Emma* (adaptation)
Douglas McGrath, 1996

Gwyneth Paltrow nails the accent in a visually lavish production, although the deeper layers from the novel are skipped over with... more archery.

1996 Oscars for best music and costume design

327

minutes of
Austen!

03 **Sense and Sensibility (adaptation)**
Ang Lee, 1995

The Emma Thompson and Kate Winslet emotional tour de force in a strong and critically acclaimed adaptation.

04 *Clueless* **(inspired by** *Emma***)**
Amy Heckerling, 1995

Probably the freshest approach to an Austen plot: *Emma* is transplanted to 1990s Los Angeles, played by an energetic Alicia Silverstone.

1995 Oscar for best screenplay

07 ***Bride and Prejudice*** **(inspired by** *Pride and Prejudice***)**
Gurinder Chadha, 2004

A contemporary Bollywood rendition that traded corsets for saris in a present-day Sikh love story. Including, as the format dictates, some great song-and-dance numbers.

08 ***Pride and Prejudice and Zombies*** **(inspired by)**
Burr Steers, 2016

A comedy-satire, based on the book of the same name, which had been a runaway hit. The film bombed at the box office, despite the irresistible depiction of the character of George Wickham as a zombie from the start.

TYPOGRAPHIC AUSTEN

Chapman

carriage

John Murray

Sense & Sensibility

hot-pressed paper

universal

civility

juvenilia

Steventon

naturalism

folly

Jane

Emma

global fame

universal truth

love

provincial

spinster

writing desk

Chawton

Northanger Abbey

elegance

officers

dedication

eloquence

Mansfield Park

sofa

courtship

reprint

theatricals

BRAND AUSTEN

As one might expect of a writer with near-global popularity, Jane Austen has inspired a lot of products. Some items seem a more natural fit with the esteemed authoress than others.

01 If you want to mix up a batch of Jane cookies, there's a cutter that will not only cut them in the outline of the Cassandra Austen portrait, but will also stamp her features on them.

02 The scent of romance: Pemberley, 'A Jane Austen-inspired perfume' is promoted like this:

03 Austen's portrait first appeared on UK £10 banknotes in 2017. Ironically this is just the price paid by the first – non-publishing – publisher to purchase her first novel, *Susan*.

"DAB SOME 'PEMBERLEY' ON YOUR WRIST, LOCK ARMS WITH YOUR LOVER, AND TAKE A TURN ABOUT THE GARDEN."

04 Wounded by love? For just $7, you can plaster over the problem with a tin of 15 large bandaids featuring characters from the novels.

05

Anyone determined to add some authentic Austen romance to their wedding day can buy a box of heart-shaped confetti – cut from the pages of *Pride and Prejudice*.

06

In 2010, Google marked Jane Austen's 235th birthday with a celebratory illustration of Austen couple depicted in the English countryside.

07

If you don't want to commit your skin to a permanent dedication to Jane, temporary tattoos offering a range of her best-known quotations are available.

"*Angry people are not always wise*"

08

You can also recharge your smartphone with a charger cunningly disguised as a vintage copy of *Northanger Abbey*.

09

Give your rooms that Regency air with a Jane-themed air-freshener. It's advertised as being 'sensibly scented' – with lavender.

AUSTEN AT AUCTION

£2,300

1933
MANUSCRIPT OF *LADY SUSAN*

Passed from Cassandra Austen to her niece, Fanny Knight, and auctioned on the sale of the library of her son, Lord Braborne, in 1893. Bought for £90 by Lord Rosebery, it remained in his library until 1933 when sold to Walter M Hill, a bookseller from Chicago. Now found in the Morgan Library, New York.

£180,000

2008
PRINTED COPY OF *EMMA*

One of only 12 presentation copies produced ahead of the book's first print run. The first was given to the librarian for the Prince Regent – as requested, *Emma* was dedicated to the Regent, rather reluctantly. This copy was given to Anne Sharp, a friend of Jane's who had been governess to her brother Edward's children.

£993,250

2011
MANUSCRIPT OF *THE WATSONS*

A 68-page draft of the unfinished novel, abandoned in 1804, auctioned at Sotheby's, London.

2013
PORTRAIT OF JANE AUSTEN

Sold at Sotheby's, London, based on Cassandra Austen's drawing, and commissioned by her nephew, James Edward Austen-Leigh, to enable the publisher to make an engraved frontispiece.

£135,000

2013
JANE AUSTEN'S TURQUOISE RING

£152,450

Simple 9ct gold ring, set with a round turquoise. Purchased by the American singer Kelly Clarkson, who, after an uproar about the piece leaving the UK, later resold it to the Jane Austen House Museum in Chawton for £149,000.

2014
JANE AUSTEN'S SIGNATURE

£23,750

A high price reached at Bonhams, London, for a signature and a date – January 1811 – only, on a slip of paper evidently clipped from a book's flyleaf.

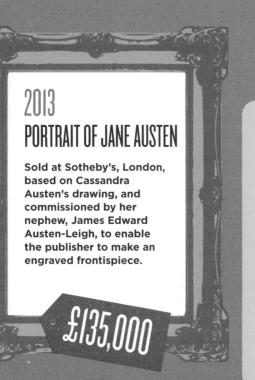

2014
PRINTED COPY OF *EMMA*

£48,050

Rare three-volume set from the first print run, still bound in its publisher's boards (most owners subsequently selected their own bindings to fit with their existing libraries).

BIOGRAPHIES

Martha Lloyd (1765–1843)
Martha and sister Mary were Jane and Cassandra Austen's greatest friends. They were daughters of Noyes Lloyd, a clergyman. Martha lived in the Austen household at Chawton and Southampton, and eventually became Francis Austen's wife.

Cassandra Austen (1773–1845)
Jane's older sister; probably the most important person in her life. Although Cassandra is most famous for having destroyed many of Austen's letters, she did much more to preserve her legacy than she did to damage it.

Reverend George Austen (1731–1805)
Jane's father, a country rector, known in his youth for his good looks, and for his calm and scholarly temperament. He encouraged her early writings and was the first to approach a publisher to see if she could reach a wider readership than the family circle.

John Murray (1778–1843)
John Murray was publisher to both Lord Byron and Sir Walter Scott, and was the best-known and most eminent publisher of Georgian London. He was first to publish Austen's four novels, *Emma, Mansfield Park, Northanger Abbey* and *Persuasion*.

Cassandra Austen, née Leigh (1739–1827)
Jane's mother, who outlived her famous daughter by a decade. She was happy in her marriage and known in her family as a lively, energetic personality and a more than capable manager of her household. Unusually, all eight of her children survived to adulthood.

Tom Lefroy (1776–1869)
Tom Lefroy is the only man for whom it is known that Jane Austen formed an affection. The nephew of the Reverend George Lefroy, he lived at Ashe, not far from Steventon. When Tom visited him there in December 1795 he and Jane became fond of one another.

Henry Austen (1771–1850)
Jane's favourite brother. His careers included serving in the militia and founding a bank, before financial disaster forced him into holy orders in 1816. He authored the 'biographical notice' in the first publication of *Northanger Abbey* and *Persuasion*.

Harris Bigg-Wither (1781–1833)
The younger brother of Alethea (only sons of the family inherited the -Wither part of the name) proposed to Austen in 1802. First accepting, she changed her mind, deciding it would be folly to marry without affection.

Alethea Bigg (1777–date of death unknown)
Alethea Bigg and her sister Catherine were girlhood friends of Jane and Cassandra Austen. They lived at Manydown Park, a handsome country house near to Steventon, and the Austen girls often paid lengthy visits there.

Francis Austen (1774–1865)
One of two of Jane's brothers who served in the Navy. Joining at the age of just 12, Francis rose steadily through the ranks, eventually becoming Admiral of the Fleet in 1863. His second wife was Martha Lloyd, Jane's great friend.

Eliza de Feuillide, née Hancock/later Austen (1761–1813)
Jane Austen's exotic cousin was the daughter of Philadelphia Hancock. Born in India and living later in both France and England, she brought glimpses of a wider and more sophisticated world to her Austen cousins.

Thomas Egerton (c. 1784–1830)
First publisher of Jane Austen's work: he brought out *Sense and Sensibility*, on commission, in 1811 (she earned £140) and *Pride and Prejudice*, for which he bought the copyright for £110, in 1813.

family   publishers

friends   suitors

INDEX

ACKNOWLEDGMENTS

Picture credits
The publishers would like to thank the following for permission to reproduce their images in this book. Every effort has been made to acknowledge copyright holders, and the publishers apologize for any omissions.

23 © iStock images.
42 Carriage Silhouettes © Shutterstock/elmm.
57 Oscar Wilde, photograph by Napoleon Sarony, 1882 © Shutterstock/Everett Historical.
71 Fanny Burney © Shutterstock/Everett Historical.
74 © iStock images.
81 Ralph Waldo Emerson, from an original drawing by Sam W. Rowse, ca.1845. © Shutterstock/Everett Historical.